Catholic Church, Diocese of Orléans

Letter From the Right Reverend the Lord Bishop of Orleans to M. Minghetti

minister of finance to King Victor Emmanuel - on the spoliation of the Church at Rome and throughout Italy

Catholic Church, Diocese of Orléans

Letter From the Right Reverend the Lord Bishop of Orleans to M. Minghetti
minister of finance to King Victor Emmanuel - on the spoliation of the Church at Rome and throughout Italy

ISBN/EAN: 9783337100858

Printed in Europe, USA, Canada, Australia, Japan

Cover: Foto ©Lupo / pixelio.de

More available books at **www.hansebooks.com**

LETTER

FROM THE RIGHT REVEREND

THE LORD BISHOP OF ORLEANS

TO

M. MINGHETTI,

MINISTER OF FINANCE TO KING VICTOR EMMANUEL,

ON THE

Spoliation of the Church

AT ROME AND THROUGHOUT ITALY.

TOGETHER WITH

*THE BRIEF OF THE POPE TO THE BISHOP OF ORLEANS
ON THE OCCASION OF THIS LETTER.*

––––––––––

LONDON: BURNS AND OATES,

PORTMAN STREET AND PATERNOSTER ROW.

1874.

LONDON :
ROBSON AND SONS, PRINTERS, PANCRAS ROAD, N.W.

PREFACE OF TRANSLATOR.

THE English press in general has represented the following Letter as only a fresh outburst of an eminent member of the Roman Catholic Church in favour of the Temporal Power, in order ' to keep alive the grievances of their chief in Italy;' which grievances they represent as purely imaginary.

A portion of the French press, on the other hand, considers that the Bishop's language is that of resignation to an accomplished fact—an impression which he himself indignantly denies.

We can only implore our readers not to be misled by these equally false though opposite statements, and not to trust to the garbled extracts from the Letter put forward in the newspapers; but to read, if possible without any preconceived prejudice, this plain and unvarnished statement of facts.

We believe that, with the strong sense of honesty and fair-play which is the inherent characteristic of all Englishmen, they will be startled beyond measure at the revelations it contains, and which we defy them to disprove; and that they will feel that the 'solution of the Roman Question' can never be arrived at by injustice and wrong, or by a direct violation of the Divine commandment, 'Thou shalt not steal.'

CONTENTS.

LETTER TO M. MINGHETTI.

Sir,—In 1848 you were the Minister of Pius IX.; I find you in 1874 the Minister of Victor Emmanuel.

You coöperated with the Holy Father in a great, fruitful, and glorious undertaking; and although to-day you lend your aid to, alas, a very different work, I know that you have retained a grateful recollection of the generous Sovereign who gave you such a proof of his esteem. Therefore it is that with a certain degree of confidence I take the liberty of addressing you this Letter.

I am just come back from Rome. I have seen with my own eyes all that is passing there. Nothing can be more sad; and I like to think that it is not without bitter regret that you are taking part in such proceedings. Everything is done with consummate skill, and with a deep meaning. There is no noise, no outward violence; everything is concealed under an apparent legality; but nevertheless, what is being done is the greatest disaster that could befall the Church, and, if she could be destroyed by the hand of man, would be her ruin.

But Europe, indifferent or distracted by other interests, appears to see nothing and to know nothing; and France, still bleeding from her late reverses, and trembling on the edge of an abyss, can do naught but mourn. The Catholic world is deceived. They even boast of the liberty which the noble Prisoner of the Vatican enjoys under your protection!

I will say more: you are deceived yourselves. You do not know all that is being done in your name; your agents (I cannot think otherwise) go beyond your instructions ; and allow me to say that they do not do you credit.

I have taken it upon myself, therefore, to let you know yourself the real state of things.

Do not, however, be afraid. I do not ignore the delicacy of such a subject, and I shall respect it ; I do not, in this Letter, make an appeal to the sword, but to justice and good faith ; I do not, either, intend to make this a party question. The subjects on which I shall touch are outside and above the arena of parties. You have solemnly declared yourselves that you would not wound the consciences of Christians, nor attempt to solve alone, but in accordance with the States possessing Catholic subjects, questions which affect the interests of the whole Catholic body. Would it be an offence to the Italian Government to remind her of her engagements and of her promises ? And is it not doing a useful as well as a loyal act to warn those who need the warning ?

Besides, if it be true, as I believe, that the actual position of things creates, not only for Catholics and for Italy, but for the whole world, a state of peril from which one may turn away for a moment in the midst of the pressing difficulties of the hour, but which we shall have to face some day or other, is it not the interest of every one, in so grave a matter, not to persevere in dangerous illusions ?

For us, Catholics of all nations, it is a duty not to conceal, by our silence, that which, under no pretext and by no country on earth, could be excused or passed over.

And for the Government of which you are the head, is it not of vital importance to take account of such things and to foresee, so as to avoid them, the disastrous complications of the future ?

I.

The Promises of the Italian Government.

Before giving an opinion on what is passing at this moment in Rome, it is important to recall the promises which the Italian Government made, and the engagements into which she entered, to respect the Church and her rights, and at the same time the rights of conscience of the Catholic world.

When, during the late war, fortune deserted our troops and betrayed our hopes, the very day when the soldiers who had the honour of guarding Rome against you were recalled, your Government understood that, having nothing more to fear from us, her hour was come ; and with a resolution which did not require much courage, she made her plans. But before executing them, she felt the need of dissipating the alarms of the Catholic body on the consequences of the attack which was about to be made ; and also to reassure the Powers whose subjects, being Catholics, had consequently vital interests at Rome.

Therefore, on the 29th August 1870, M. Visconti-Venosta, your Minister of Foreign Affairs, addressed a *memorandum* or circular to all Italian agents at foreign Courts, of which we give the textual conclusions :

‘ The Government PROMISES to preserve ALL THE INSTITUTIONS, offices, and ecclesiastical bodies existing at Rome, as well as those employed therein.

‘ The Government PROMISES to *preserve intact*, and without submitting them to special taxation, ALL ECCLESIASTICAL PROPERTIES, of which the revenues belong to offices, CORPORATIONS, institutions, and ecclesiastical bodies having their seat in Rome and in the Leonine city.’

Thus everything was to be respected by you and preserved —*entirely* preserved—both the possession of property and the position of persons. Such were your engagements and your promises. Nothing could be more formal or more solemn ; for these words were addressed to all the Courts of Europe.

The memorandum went on to say :

‘ The Government will not meddle with the internal discipline of the *ecclesiastical corporations in Rome*. The bishops and priests of the kingdom are free, in their respective dioceses and parishes, of *all interference from the Government* in the exercise of their spiritual functions.’

But this is not all. To give a more emphatic guarantee to the Catholic world, the memorandum made the following declaration :

‘ These articles shall be considered as A PUBLIC AND BILATERAL CONTRACT, AND THE POINT OF UNION WITH THE POWERS HAVING CATHOLIC SUBJECTS.’

The Italian Government went still further; and some days before the invasion, the 6th of September, you put forward a manifesto, in which you stated that you had at last decided to enter Rome. But why? '*Not to abandon the fate of the Head of the Church to the chapter of accidents.*' Such was your solicitude.

It was in analogous terms, and with equal sincerity (how can we evade the comparison?), that M. de Cavour, on the eve of Castelfidardo, proclaimed to Europe, in another famous memorandum, that he only wished to '*cross the Pontifical territory* TO DEFEND IT FROM THE REVOLUTION against which he was about to fight on Neapolitan soil.'

It was thus again that, in concluding the convention of the 15th of September, to remove your capital to Florence, you proclaimed that you would not enter Rome save by '*moral influences.*' Doubtless they were such as were used by your generals on the 20th of September to throw down the walls of Rome and to force the Porta Pia.

It was thus, in fact, that at the very beginning of this war in Italy, the object from the first hour of such well-founded alarm in all Catholic hearts, the Emperor himself declared solemnly, and reiterated the declaration by the mouth of his Ministers to the episcopate and the deputies, that this war was not undertaken ' to shake the Pontifical throne, which we ourselves have reëstablished; and that ALL THE RIGHTS OF THE TEMPORAL SOVEREIGNTY OF THE POPE would be respected.'

But the Italian Government felt herself the more stringently bound to reiterate these assurances to the Powers and the Catholic body, which had been so often deceived, from the fact that her precedents, her principles, her laws, her acts, all this war which since 1848 she had not ceased to direct against the clergy and the Church, had only too naturally excited the most violent suspicions of her intentions. M. de Cavour, in derision, had adopted this maxim: 'A free Church in a free State.' Now this is what he had already done with the Church and its liberty:

All Church property had been confiscated; all religious orders suppressed; thousands of religious despoiled and hunted down; the nuns turned out of their convents night after night by the carabineers, and left in the street—' I thank God,' writes one superior, ' that none of my sisters perished in the high-road ;' bishops and archbishops, including the Archbishops of Turin and Cagliari and many others, thrown into prison.

Bishoprics left vacant by the hundred ; the concordat with the Holy See violated ; all ecclesiastical immunities, stipulated in a treaty with Rome, abolished.

The Siccardi law voted, to the cry of ' Down with the priests !'

The marriage law voted on the 5th of June 1852, in spite of the Pope, in spite of the concordat, in spite of the bishops.

The law of the 25th November 1854, formally violating against the Church the 29th art. of the national statute : ' All property, WITHOUT ANY EXCEPTION, is inviolable.'

In vain from the tribune a former Minister of the King, Charles Albert reminded the Government that these words, ' WITHOUT ANY EXCEPTION,' which are not to be found in any other Constitution, were added to the statute by the King himself, and precisely with the object of protecting ecclesiastical property. In vain, pointing to the statue of Charles Albert, he exclaimed : ' Certainly, gentlemen, if the King Charles Albert, whose statue is before your eyes, could have foreseen how to-day you dare to interpret his intentions and his acts, he would have drawn back that hand stretched out to swear to the Constitution. Yes, gentlemen, he would indignantly have withdrawn it !' Noble but fruitless words. The law was voted.

And what you did in Piedmont, you hastened to do in all the provinces violently annexed. And all this work of spoliation was crowned and consummated by the following four laws :

7th July 1866. Law regarding religious corporations and on the conversion of real property belonging to ecclesiastical institutions.

15th August 1867. Law on the liquidation of the dominions of the Church.

27th July 1868. Law as to the pensions to be granted to the members of suppressed religious corporations.

Lastly, 11th August 1870. Law on the conversion of the property of the parishes and ecclesiastical fabrics.

I must not omit, either, the law which subjects the clergy to military conscription, and renders recruiting for the priesthood almost impossible.

I am assured, sir, that as deputy you have not voted for all these measures. But still, as Minister and President of the Council, you enforce them. And this is what makes me, in this Letter, appeal to your honour and good faith.

Such, then, were your laws, your acts, your precedents, and your fidelity to your promises. That is why, before the invasion of Rome, to prevent the stupor into which the whole Catholic world was about to be thrown by this last act of aggression, you hastened to make the solemn declarations which I have quoted above. And after the invasion, you again renewed your promises.

Thus, when the plébiscite took place as usual under the pressure of your arms, the King solemnly accepted this plébiscite ; but in accepting it, what does he do? He declares that ' the firm resolution of the Government is to *guarantee, by efficacious and lasting means*, the liberty and spiritual independence of the Holy See.'*

Very soon came the question of elections and the proposal to remove the Italian Parliament to Rome. In proposing to the King the convocation of the new Chamber, the Government reminded him of the promise we have just read, and added themselves :

' This ROYAL PROMISE was a confirmation of the votes of the Italian Parliament and of the declarations made, both before and after the entry of the Italian troops into Rome, by your Majesty's Government to the Sovereign Pontiff and TO THE CATHOLIC POWERS.'

' The Italian Government,' they continue, ' wished to justify the expectation of Europe AND THE CONFIDENCE OF THE CATHOLIC WORLD.'†

One reproach especially, which wounds them to the quick, and which they are determined to clear themselves from at

* Words quoted in setting forth the motion of the ' *Project*' of extending to Rome the laws cited above, *presented to the Chamber of Deputies in the sitting of the 20th November* 1872, *by the Minister De Falco, together with the rest of the Ministry.*

† ' Rispondere alla fiducia d' Europa e all' aspettazione del mondo Cattolico.' Ibid. p. 2.

any price, is, lest 'this great fact of the *deliverance* of Rome,' as they dare to call it (' *codesto grande fatto della liberazione di Roma*'), should be considered as a trick of the Italian Exchequer to lay violent hands on the property of the Roman Church (*una ripresa del fisco*). They declare again, in consequence, that 'the patrimony of the Roman Church shall remain intact in the hands of the Church,—*Il patrimonio della Chiesa Romana rimarrà intero alla Chiesa.*'*

The new Parliament met. At the sitting of the 30th January 1871, M. Visconti-Venosta did not forget to renew his assurances to the Catholic world in these terms :

' We have always declared that we wished to solve the Roman question WITHOUT OFFENDING THE FEELINGS OF CA-THOLICS *and the legitimate interests of other Governments.*'

Finally, to give a last and unanswerable proof of your sincerity, you hastened, sir, to draw up your famous *Law of Guarantees*, in which you once more proclaimed the entire liberty of the Sovereign Pontiff.

This, then, is what the Italian Government promised and hoped to persuade the world of : *i.e.* that under your domination the Pope would remain free ; that his spiritual government would in no way be hindered or interfered with ; that at Rome, ecclesiastical corporations and their property would be religiously preserved : in a word, that all Catholic interests would be respected !

Such were your engagements and your promises. Now let us see what are your acts.

II.

Spoliation of the Church. Liquidation of Ecclesiastical Property.

Well, sir, your good faith will not allow you to deny that, after such solemn promises, what the Piedmontese brought to Rome and the Pope—strange liberators !—has been, in reality, spoliation, oppression, and ruin.

In fact, having once taken these precautions to blind public opinion, which is so ready to believe in fine phrases, and trusting to the weakness of political consciences, who only

* Ibid. p. 3.

wish to be deceived, you set to work cleverly and legally, and gave yourself full swing.

The first thing which your Chamber of Deputies did was to vote (and your Senate to sanction, and your King to promulgate) a law which applies to Rome and to all the patrimony of St. Peter—the laws of the 7th July 1866, 15th August 1867, 29th July 1868, and 11th August 1870; that is, the whole masterpiece of legislative spoliation which deprives the Church of her property, disperses her secular patrimony, confiscates all her goods, destroys her religious corporations, and annihilates her very constitution.

And the same law instituted a *giunta* called *liquidatrice*, which silently and implacably pursues the work of spoliation by which your Government pretends 'to justify the expectation of Europe AND THE CONFIDENCE OF THE CATHOLIC WORLD.' Thus you, having promised to respect and preserve everything, the whole ecclesiastical body with its organisation and its property—you have confiscated, upset, and destroyed everything.

And now, at the present moment, what does the Church possess in Rome?

Nothing; the Pope does not even possess St. Peter's or the Vatican; not even the little chapel where he says Mass; not even the room where he lives.

People said: *The Vatican is a garden.* We have come to that. But even the Vatican and its gardens do not belong to the Pope, but to you. He occupies them merely at your will and pleasure. He is living there as a lodger and a stranger in that palace built by the Popes, and still filled with the majesty of their secular sovereignty.

Besides this, he can no longer set foot in Rome. Do not say that your laws do not forbid him to do so. Your very presence at Rome forbids it! Can he expose his sacred person to tumultuous manifestations, such as we have witnessed only a few days ago, where cries of death echoed against him even to the threshold of the Vatican?

Such, then, is the actual position of the Pope and the Church in this Rome, where you entered into a solemn engagement to preserve everything. The person of the Pope is in your hands; the Sacred College is in your hands; the future Conclave is in your hands.

But more than this:

From the Sovereign Pontiff down to the humblest ecclesiastic in the poorest church in Rome, everything is at your mercy; the daily bread of all the clergy depends upon you; Pope, cardinals, bishops, priests, all are, as far as regards their material subsistence, under the yoke of your finance; a revolution, a war, a movement of caprice in your Chambers, and all the Roman clergy may be, in one moment, reduced to utter mendicity.

Ah, it affronts you, Italian Ministers, that we should call 'the great fact of the liberation of Rome' a seizure by your Exchequer of the property of the Church! But you must own, sir, that if I were to call things by their right names, I should have to use a shorter and plainer word.

Such are the laws that have been passed and to this state are we arrived; and then you dare to declare that the patrimony of the Roman Church shall remain intact in the hands of the Church: '*Il patrimonio della Chiesa Romana rimarrà intero alla Chiesa!*' It is true that you add, in order to save appearances, 'excepting, be it understood, the application of our judicial principles relating to the personalty of religious associations, and also such *as may be imposed upon us by our* PECUNIARY NECESSITIES.'*

Which means, in plain English, the patrimony of the Roman Church will remain intact in the hands of the Church except that we mean to upset it altogether, and appropriate it to our own use whenever we find it convenient, and we will intrust the operation to a *giunta liquidatrice* (*la giunta liquidatrice dell' asse ecclesiastico*), who will do the work thoroughly and well.

In truth, I will do the 'giunta' the justice to say that she has in no way disappointed your hopes.

But then, sir, as Minister, you should have said frankly: 'The ecclesiastical property of Rome and of its province is as necessary to us as the ecclesiastical property of the rest of Italy. We shall do at Rome as we have done elsewhere. We shall take everything.'

* 'Fermo però, s' intende, l' applicazione dei nostri principi giuridici intorno alla personalità delle associazioni religiose, e salve le necessità economiche.' *Progetto di Legge*, p. 3.

You speak of the necessity of abolishing the mortmain act and the inalienability of property, so as to encourage, as you say, 'the fruitful transformations of industrial emulation and free trade, to people the Roman Campagna,* and to make it more healthy.' Vain pretexts! Who does not see the result? The restrictions which may be brought to bear, in the interest of industry and commerce, on the inalienability of property and mortmain, have nothing in common with what you are doing by an arbitrary dispossession, which utterly destroys the rights and liberties of the proprietor, and takes away from him at the same time the right to regulate the conditions of the sale of his goods, to fix their price, or to guarantee the use to be made of them; while, as we shall shortly see, it involves, under the lying title of *previous claims*, a spoliation of one-third of his property; that is to say, a real confiscation of a large portion, which is all the more odious when masked under the veil of hypocrisy.

Who can pretend to explain, either, how such an expropriation can be made to apply not only to agricultural lands, but to buildings, to furniture, to libraries, to archives—to things, in fact, of which the use is identified with the functions and missions of the proprietor, and thus constitute an essential condition of his life? Here it is not a question of certain agricultural improvements; it is the ruin of existing institutions.

As to 'other financial necessities,' one knows well enough this pretext of all dictatorships, which is as old as it is iniquitous. Certainly, it is bad enough to have arrived at an overburdened taxation which one is forced to bear, when an equitable partition is made, pressing equally on all citizens in a state; but to strike, as you are doing, exclusively the bodies and institutions which you have sworn to respect, and with blows which fall only on them, and which end in utter ruin, is to tear aside even the most transparent veils, and lay bare a system of proscription of persons and spoliation of property unknown in any other country.

* 'Le necessità economiche che non consentono la continuazione della manomorta e l' inalienabilità dei predii, e più specialmente dei predii rustici, che continuando a rimanere sostratti alle feconde transformazioni del libero commercio e della emulazione industriale, perpetuerebbero l'insalubrità e il disertamento delle Campagne Romane.' Ibid.

' To encourage industry and commerce, and to people and make the Roman Campagna healthy.' If that were all you wished for, why not leave the duty and give the time to the Church herself to convert her landed property into securities of another sort, which she could herself have possessed and administered?

But no; you were bent on something more. You were determined to take everything: *Una ripresa del fisco.* Italian unity being a gulf in which all the resources of Italy are being swallowed up, you must have money; still more money; always money; and to get it, in spite of your protest, in face of the whole world, that the patrimony of the Roman Church should remain intact in the hands of the Church, your Exchequer has swallowed up all: *Ripresa del fisco.* Let us look into the details.

III.

Suppression of the Religious Orders. What becomes of their Persons.

To calumniate your victims before striking them, that is a well-known revolutionary proceeding; the Religious Orders could not escape it.

I shall not pause to refute these calumnies, miserable revivals of the slanders of the last century, but which no respectable journalist would dare repeat in these days. In your position, however, you could not fail to have recourse to them. Your reporters, allow me to tell you, sir, as a Minister, are in general poor philosophers; but the reporter of the law on the suppression of religious corporations, M. Restelli, has certainly carried away the palm. Thus this honourable deputy proclaims, himself, the innumerable services rendered to humanity by the religious orders—by their works of charity, of education, of science; he owns that in periods of national calamity they powerfully concurred in saving civilisation; but at the same time, by a rare confusion of mind, it pleases him to declare* that it is in the name of this very

---

* 'I servigi resi all' umanità dalle corporazioni religiose applicate alla beneficenza, all' istruzione, ed ai studi severi, che concorsero, in epoche calamitose, a salvare la civiltà. . . . *Ora è in nome di questa stessa civiltà progressa* che il potere civile ne reclama l' abolizione.' *Relazione della Commissione. Tornata del* 3 *Aprile* 1873.

civilisation that they must be abolished. He allows that monastic vows are *the perfection of Christian virtue ;* but he pretends, at the same time, that they are also *the antithesis of all progress, material, moral, and intellectual.** M. Restelli concludes, therefore, that all religious orders should be abolished, and that all their properties should be confiscated.

But if such were your principles and your projects, why did you proclaim, before your entry into Rome, what I have before stated : ' The Government *engages itself to preserve all the institutions, offices, and* ECCLESIASTICAL BODIES *existing in Rome*' ?

Why have you sworn, in your fundamental statute, that ' All property, WITHOUT ANY EXCEPTION, was inviolable' ?

Why did you write in your Law of Guarantees : 'The Pope cannot accomplish alone the functions of his spiritual ministry, and the Church is NECESSARILY a secular body, SERVED BY REGULAR ORDERS' ?

Why do you speak, in your memorandum of the 29th of August, of a '*contract*' both ' PUBLIC AND BILATERAL, AN AGREEMENT WITH ALL POWERS POSSESSING CATHOLIC SUBJECTS' ?

And having entered into such engagements in face of existing Powers, how is it that you have thus hastened, before everything else, to apply to Rome the law which, with one blow, suppresses the religious corporations and confiscates all their goods ?

Ah, sir, I assure you that when one is thrown, as I am, by circumstances and against my will, into the arena of politics, and that one has been accustomed to live in the truth and honesty of private life, one is utterly stupefied at meeting such things on one's path.

Well, then—terrible hecatomb !—thousands of religious of both sexes in Italy, struck down by your laws, found themselves suddenly torn from these secular asylums of piety, science, and charity which they had themselves founded, and where they had the right to live and die. At Rome alone 126 monasteries of men gave shelter to 2375 religious ; 90 convents of women, 2183 nuns. Your agents, a brutal soldiery, ravaged these venerable asylums ; and the cry of the proscriptions of

---

* ' Le più perfette seconda la dottrina Cattolica . . . l' antitese di ogni progresso materiale, morale, ed intellettuale dell' uomo.' *Relazione,* &c.

old times has again been heard : ' *Hæc mea sunt, veteres migrate coloni !*' And they were compelled to turn out : to tear themselves from their peaceful sanctuaries, and to give you up everything. And there they are at this very day, dispersed, wandering, taking shelter where they can in the houses which charity has opened to receive them.

More cunning than your predecessors of the French Revolution, you endeavoured, I know, to temper your spoliation. After having robbed these religious whom you threw into the street of all that was their own, you were obliged to recognise that you had a duty of honour and justice towards them : ' *Un debito di giustizia e d' onore.*'*

Justice and honour ! Fine words and great things. Let us see how they have been understood by the Italian Government, and what 'justice and honour' induce you to give to enable those persons to live whom you have turned out of their homes, and from whom you have taken everything they possessed.

To the professed members of the Mendicant Orders you give 250 francs a year, or a little more than 50 centimes a day;† to the lay brothers of the same orders 144 francs a year, or even 96 francs, that is 25 centimes a day, according to their age.

When offering them so ridiculously inadequate a means of subsistence, you might perhaps have imagined that they would throw themselves on the charity of the public. But at the very same time your police laws forbid their having recourse to it, and you punish begging in the name of social morality :‡ *abitudine dannosa nei rispetti della moralità sociale.* Well, then, in the name of ' social morality,' let them die of hunger or get out of it as best they may.

As to the lay brothers of the Non-mendicant Orders, you expect them to live, in the midst of the daily increasing dearness of every article of consumption, at the rate (according to their ages) of 300, 240, and 200 francs a year. For the choir

---

* *Relazione della Commissione,* &c. p. 7, s. 9.

† Every one knows that a franc is tenpence of our English money, and that 100 centimes go to a franc. So that their pittance is fivepence a day for the professed monks and twopence-halfpenny for the lay brothers. *Note of Translator.*

‡ ' Le leggi di polizia, impedendo la public questua.' *Progetto di Legge,* p. 7.

monks and nuns, if they be sixty years of age or above it, they are to receive 600 francs a year; if they be from forty to sixty years old, 480 francs, and these, even when they have attained the age of sixty, are not to receive any more; while if they be under forty they are only to get 360 francs a year, or less than a franc a day.*

And no matter what amount you have taken from them. The monks of the Chartreuse at Pisa had large possessions, three parts of which at least went to the poor. This monastery was the Providence of the country. Well, you have robbed them of everything. They were very numerous at the moment of their suppression; one or two only have been left to guard the house. Well, these poor religious, to whom you tender the miserable pittance I have quoted above, if they wish to eke out their wretched subsistence by taking a few vegetables from their own kitchen-garden, must pay you for them.

Until now, this garden was their own; now it is yours, and you think it just to make them pay for what is their own, and which you have taken from them. If it be justice, I will say nothing; but if it be worthy of your agents, certainly, sir, it is unworthy of you.

O, your new system of taxation forgets nothing; of that I am well aware. But judge for yourself. Amidst all these despoiled and homeless priests, a great number depend upon a small emolument for saying masses in order to exist at all, and many of them have not even that resource. Well, on the miserable sum given to the poorest of these priests for his mass, you impose a tax. Even of this last resource in his extremity your fiscal authorities claim the lion's share. But if he should say his mass for nothing, or if he should not say it at all? No matter, *he must pay as if he said it.* The tax-gatherer supposes that a priest says mass every day, and generally for some kind of payment, saving a few days in the year. For all the other days, whether he has said mass or not, with or without salary, he must pay the tax, and this is the way your tax-collectors understand it. Is it not almost unbelievable? I was even told that one of these poor priests, who, from time to time, says mass in a private house belonging

* Regio decreto per la suppressione degli ordini e corporazioni religiose, 7 Luglio 1866, art. 3.

to a Frenchman whose name was mentioned to me, and who invited him on these occasions to take his place at his table afterwards, had been forced to pay for these occasional invitations what you call the family tax of 26 francs, on what your fiscal authorities were pleased to consider his 'revenue.' In spite of the solemn affirmation made to me of this fact, I really doubt it still.

Another enormity. There are about 120 bishops from whom everything has been robbed, houses and goods, and who receive nothing from you, not even the pension awarded to lay brothers. The Pope gives them an alms of 500 francs a month. Certainly, if anything should escape the grasp of your taxation, it would be the help which comes from Peter's pence, which is a twice-told alms, the alms of the Pope and our own. Well, on this very alms each bishop is compelled to pay you a tax.

But now let us mention another case which is of frequent occurrence. Among these monks and nuns, there are many of them who have brought a large dowry, that is, their own private fortune, to their convent. In that case, what course was pointed out to you by *justice and honour?* Doubtless it would occur to you that, when you sent them back to a secular life, you would restore to them the fortunes which belonged to them, as much as your own income belongs to you. But no; these private fortunes are confiscated like all the rest, and you do not scruple to turn *their* owners into the street, with the miserable handful of francs I have quoted above.

This injustice is so glaring and the proofs so evident that you yourselves have inserted in your law an exception for those who have been professed since 1864.* But why not for the others? Is not the reason identical and the injustice the same for all? This is not a question of ecclesiastical property; it is a question of the rights of families, the legitimate possessors of which properties are before your eyes, and to whom the most vulgar notion of what is called *justice and honour* among honest men commands the restitution of that which is their own.

There is at this moment going on in Rome a famous trial, which brings to light one of the most revolting preten-

---

* Regio decreto, art. 5.

sions of your fiscal system. A member of a religious community, thinking himself at the point of death, made a gift
to the community. The said community was dissolved, and
its goods confiscated; but the religious did not die. Naturally, when he was turned out of his convent, he claimed the
money he had given, not to the Government, but to his community. But no; the Government pretends that everything
belongs to them, and refuse to give back to the poor monk
his own private property.*

But are the rights of private property, even independently
of convents, respected by your fiscal system? The land and
buildings of the Pretorian Camp did not belong to any community, but to a private individual—to that noble and generous
Mgr. de Mérode, whom death has so prematurely and so sadly
torn from the Church. Up to his last moment, he paid you
the taxes on this ground; but you seized all, both the tax and
the camp.

Among these poor monks of so many different orders, there
were the old, infirm, sick, and blind. What have you done with
them? You have discovered an economical way of keeping
them alive; and I was a witness in Rome of the saddest possible
sight, which takes place in the Capuchin convent near the
Palazzo Barberini. There you have gathered, or rather
huddled together, all the old and infirm members of the different religious communities in Rome. They have been
dragged, in spite of their tears and protestations, from the
homes where they lived under a rule of their own choice, and
where they had certainly purchased the right to die by a long
life of labour, penance, and prayer. And now they are dying
of misery, neglect, and desolation in this hospital of your in-
vention, far from all those who loved them, and who were
the companions of their whole existence.

Thus, then, all this grand religious life in Rome, where
you so solemnly promised to respect it, is destroyed; all
these creations of Christian centuries are annihilated.

You say, it is true, that, although you cannot recognise
the religious life, nothing in your laws forbids it, and that the
corporations you have dissolved as moral bodies may revive
again under another form.

* Il sacerdote Luigi Carlini contra la giunta liquidatrice.

But they have nothing left belonging to them, these un-happy corporations ; you have taken everything from them ; how, then, and with what means are they to revive again ?

Centuries of toil, prodigies of economy, sobriety, and self-devotion, had been needed to create them. You rob them of all, and say to them : ' Of what do you complain ? You have the same virtues, the same chances ; begin again ! You have been centuries about it ? Well, you will be centuries more.'

But in the liquidation of ecclesiastical property at least, has no share been given to them ? No ; none.

We have seen what has become of the persons ; now let us see what has become of the goods of the Religious Orders.

IV.

Suppression of the Religious Orders. What becomes of their Goods.

The spoliation of the Religious Orders is complete, ab-solute. All—houses, gardens, museums, libraries, archives, rare objects of art ; all those treasures of religion, science, art, antiquity—all have been carried away from their monas-teries. You have now the power of disposing of everything.*

And there is no doubt that you look sharply after your gains, and leave out nothing.

Have you not constantly had law-suits with religious for some little thing which you fancy they have concealed?—a book, an ornament, a reliquary—some little remembrance which was dear to them ?

Have we not seen at Assisi a whole army of police de-spatched after a poor lay brother, who was accused of having concealed some articles which had belonged to his monastery? The house was surrounded, the lay brother seized and thrown into prison with great indignities, and finally released ; the poor brother had never hidden anything at all !

Have I not read in the Italian newspapers that at Bo-logna, in spite of the 24th art. of your law of 7th July 1866, all the furniture of the church of St. Dominic was sold by public auction—chasubles, busts of saints, even the sacred vessels themselves ?

* Decreto regio del 7 Luglio 1866, art. 24.

The archives of the Chartreuse at Pisa, which go back to the tenth century, are equally menaced with destruction.

Two hundred thousand volumes were contained in the magnificent library of the learned monks of the monastery of the Minerva ; what will it please you to do with them ?

Less rich, perhaps, but still magnificent also, was the Library Vallicelliana, in itself a *chef-d'œuvre* of art, possessing 40,000 volumes and 3000 manuscripts. It is there that the sons of St. Philip Neri preserve the private library of their holy founder, including 300 volumes *annotated by him;* this library, which has remained as it is since the days of Baronius—have you not tried to destroy it altogether, and to divide the space into ten rooms, to be filled with I know not what ?

The other day I went all over this magnificent convent of St. Philip's Oratory, where at every turn one comes upon recollections so dear to piety and religion. In a distant corner, at which one arrives with difficulty by low doors and back staircases, are huddled together a few of the members of the old community, who have been allowed to remain there out of tolerance. It is in that usurped home, invaded by force, and under the very eyes of its ancient possessors, that you have installed your law courts and administer *justice.*

I saw the crowd of pleaders which filled the cloisters. Well, sir, allow me to tell you that if I were your procurator-general, in the name of the seventh commandment—*non furaberis*—in that very house, the scene of your own robberies, I should begin by demanding justice against yourselves.

And so many other incomparable libraries, treasures of science sacred and profane—the scenes of our studies and our toil, which our popes and cardinals and monks had created and added to with such genius and patience ; do you think that we can see these pass into your hands without the greatest sadness and the most well-founded alarm?

Will not the day come, and that before long, when, with ancient chalices and valuable pictures, the Italian Government, more and more straitened for means, will sell them all to England ?

And what will you do with the cloisters invaded by your agents ?

I saw at Naples the celebrated Chartreuse, that admirable monastery which all Europe has visited, on that beautiful mountain in front of Vesuvius and of that glistening sea. Formerly a gentle and benevolent monk received the traveller, offered him refreshment, and showed him over the monastery with kindness and intelligence. Now a rough soldier receives you and conducts you over the place, making ridiculous efforts to make his bad French understood. Instead of the magnificent library, which has been carried off and thrown no one knows where, they have placed there a shop of Venetian glass and painted crockery. Such is the progress of civilisation! Of the thirty-two monks who were there, two only have been permitted to remain, who wander sadly in the solitude of their desecrated and desolate cloisters. No longer do the praises of God rise up to heaven in hymns and spiritual songs; the choir is deserted. No venerable white-robed monks remain to walk majestically under those magnificent porticoes, or to rise and pray during the splendour of those Neapolitan nights for the great and populous city sleeping at the foot of the holy mountain.

Thus had religion, poetry, and art sanctified all the heights, all the valleys, and all the most beautiful sites of this lovely Italy. On all sides prayer and praise, in uninterrupted accents, rose up to the throne of God. In its solitary places, as in its cities, the soul of man found everywhere holy shelters for lives of love and disinterested charity, for tranquil study or for the devotion and self-abnegation of the apostolate. All these noble creations of Catholic faith on this Christian soil have disappeared or are disappearing. The walls are not yet all cast down, but their soul is gone. Life is extinct. They have left neither religion, nor poetry, nor art, nor truth—nothing!

L'Ara Cœli, that monument of the victory of the Saviour over Jupiter Capitolinus, has been transformed into a guard-house. On those steps the butt-end of the soldier's musket replaces the monk's sandal. Here again is a fine instance of progress.

Those admirable cloisters of Michael Angelo at the Baths of Diocletian, what have they done with them? Those pure, grand, simple lines have been broken and dishonoured.

They talk of turning the magnificent church of the Gesù into a great theatre, and the church of St. Ignatius into a chamber of commerce.

Those venerated cells of St. Ignatius, St. Louis of Gonzagua, of St. Stanislas Kotska, St. Philip Neri ; those recollections of St. Ambrose, St. Jerome, St. Francis of Assisi, St. Dominic, and so many others—what will become of them ?

There are churches in Italy which have already been turned into stables. Is it believable ? And when the day comes, which is too surely approaching, alas ! when, the Italian and Roman clergy being so greatly diminished by the suppression of the religious orders and so many other causes, you will find there are too many churches in Italy and at Rome, what devastation, what profanations may we not expect !

For what religious remembrance or associations will ever stop you ?

What have you done with the Coliseum itself ? that earth, bathed in the blood of countless martyrs, of which one of our popes gathered up the dust to send it to an emperor of Germany who had asked him for some relics, saying : ' You wish for relics ? See, here they are. Here, even the very dust is sacred !' By the hand of a forgetful and ungrateful archæologist, you have thrown down the venerated Way of the Cross; you have profaned the soil with useless excavations, and you have gratuitously wounded the piety of the whole Catholic world.

Do you not also assert that the Catacombs are yours ? The Church, then, can no longer descend freely even into the Catacombs! The Catacombs, her dearest treasure, her cradle, the place of sepulture of her martyrs, the sanctuary of the most heroic memories, which paganism itself respected, which all generations of Christians have visited on their knees, you are to dispose of them at your will ?

Let you alone, and it will soon be true that *Rome is no longer Rome*. Christian Rome, all her religious character, is rapidly disappearing in your greedy hands.

And then you say that you wish ' to SOLVE THE ROMAN QUESTION *without wounding the* FEELINGS *of Catholic nations'* or BETRAYING OUR TRUST' ? I ask you yourself, in the name of honour and good faith, is it *that* which you are doing ?

You have been forced, it is true, to consent to some exceptions; and there are one or two ecclesiastical bodies, the chapters, for instance, and certain colleges, which you have not been able to suppress. Well, what have you done with them?

You cannot suppress, but you ruin them by the application of your new laws.

You put up their property to auction, and you insist that a sale shall be effected within three years for country and two years for town property.

Disastrous conditions, which inevitably inflict on the sellers incalculable losses, in consequence of the quantity of land brought all at once into the market, and with so brief a delay, as well as by the greedy manœuvres of the companies interested in the sales.

Thus in the last few days you have forced a compulsory sale of the property of ten separate chapters.

And with the capital thus realised, to be converted into nominal Italian funds, what do they do? First, they take a third, 30 per cent, for right of transfer; then, another third from the accumulation of previous deductions; then the house-tax of about 13 per cent, if the establishment be for the aged poor; still further, a tax of 2 per cent if the property be mortmain, or 5 per cent if it is not, without counting the ordinary cadastral tax in the exceptional cases where the non-suppressed establishments have preserved any landed property.

In a word, enormous losses on the price of the property by the ruinous conditions of the sale, besides *a reduction of two-thirds of the price of the sale* by repeated previous deductions; thus do you fulfil your declared promise of the *exemption of ecclesiastical property from all special charges.* And you still dare to affirm, in your explanation of the motives of these laws, that they leave entire to the Roman Church the patrimony of the Church: IL PATRIMONIO DELLA CHIESA RIMARRÀ INTERO ALLA CHIESA.

I ask you, sir, as a Minister, is not your sincerity thereby deeply compromised?

V.

Foundations of Catholic Nations—the Disasters which the Italian Laws inflict upon them.

What, perhaps, is one of the strangest features in all this, and the most opposed to the engagements entered into by the Italian Government *vis-à-vis* Catholic nations, is her pretension of applying this despoiling legislation even to the establishments which these nations have founded in Rome, and which belong to them, and which you cannot despoil without violating—this must be clearly understood—not only natural justice, but the strictest international rights.

Who does not know it, sir? Rome is the common home of all Catholics. ' This Rome,' said Montaigne long ago, ' deserves our affection, united as it is for so many ages and by so many titles to our crown. It is the common and metropolitan city of all Christian nations, Spanish or French ; each finds himself at home there. To be members of that state it is only needful to belong to Christianity wherever it may exist. There is no spot here below on which Heaven has showered such favours and such constancy.'

Therefore it is that all Catholic nations of the Old and New World have fixed themselves at Rome—English, Belgians, Germans, Spaniards, Americans, all nations, in fact; and France—and it is our glory and our pride—figures in the foremost rank. We possess, therefore, in this city certain *pious foundations :* St. Louis des Français, founded by Catherine of Medicis ; St. Claude des Bourguignons ; St. Nicolas des Lorrains ; St. Ives des Bretons, the Purification of four nations ; St. Saviour's *in thermis :* all houses administered by our ambassador, by means of a commission. We have also a number of *religious houses :* the French Seminary ; the Chartreux, at St. Mary of the Angels ; the Lazarists, established at Rome by the Duchesse d'Aiguillon ; our brave Trappists, who have made more healthy, though at the risk of their lives—and many have died—the deadly plains of St. Paul at the Three Fountains ; without counting a number of houses of brothers and sisters. Independently of other expenses which they have to meet, the administration of the *pious foundations* distributes annually from 30,000 to 40,000 francs to succour such poor or sick French people as may be living in or passing through Rome.

Well, these French foundations you have, in the first place, taxed enormously. Under Pius IX. they paid 11,500 francs. To-day they have to pay 28,000 francs—nearly three times as much; and they are threatened with a payment of 34,000 francs. But more than this: all these foreign houses, pious foundations, and communities you want to submit also to your new system of forced sales in two years, and for right of transfer to take from them 30 per cent!

But do you not see that it is the money of Catholic nations which in this way, sir, you would appropriate?

But property which has been bought with charges beyond its value does not even stop you. The Trappists of St. Paul at the Three Fountains, to whom Pius IX. confided that unhealthy tract of land to try and improve it—so unhealthy, as I before mentioned, that many have died in the attempt; and who are obliged each year to leave their monastery for three months—these Trappists, I repeat, bought with their savings (to escape from the malaria of that deadly season) a house near St. John Lateran. Well, the Government want them to sell it, and to take, be it understood, the third of the price of the sale, and squeeze out of the remainder the previous deductions we have before mentioned. The Chartreux, for their house at St. Mary of the Angels, have spent an enormous sum, granted to them *on loan* (of which they have the title-deeds) by the great Chartreuse in France. In the same way the Chartreuse of Pavia, closed for a long while, but reopened in 1843 by the French Chartreux, has been also taken possession of by you. They have not yet obtained permission to touch their own funds. Well, these too, sir, are French funds, which do not belong to you in any way whatever.

And then you talk, in your memorandum of the 29th of August, of 'AN AGREEMENT OR UNION WITH THE POWERS possessing in Rome Catholic subjects.' Where, then, is this agreement or union? Now you pretend that the Government and the Italian Parliament are alone qualified to decide these imperial interests, which concern the Catholics of the whole world.

But this is not all. And you seize that which, from other and graver reasons, does not belong to you in the least.

VI.

The ancient origin and international character of the principal riches of the Roman Church.

It is not only Rome, it is the Catholic world which you are robbing.

Rome is the universal country, the capital, not of Italy, but of the whole Catholic world; and it is to the Catholic world that she owes, in a great measure, her riches and her splendour. And to begin with, do there exist in the whole world possessions more ancient, more consecrated by centuries, than those of the Roman Church? Only the other day, in his last *Bulletin Archéologique*, that illustrious and learned man, M. de Rossi, described two stone monuments attesting 'the very ancient origin of this patrimony of the Roman Church, which,' he adds—'maintained for sixteen centuries, amidst a thousand vicissitudes, until these latter days—is now sold by auction before our very eyes.'

Thus the barbarians and conquerors of the Middle Ages, revolutions and wars, have passed over Rome, and the patrimony of the Church has always been respected. It was reserved to the Italian Government to consummate this sacrilegious spoliation.

St. John Lateran, for instance, the Pope's cathedral, built by Constantine, and secularly honoured as the head and mistress of all churches (*omnium ecclesiarum mater et caput*), and the metropolis of the Catholic world, of what does its property consist? Of foundations the most ancient, the most illustrious, and the most uncontestable in the whole world.

It is, perhaps, a unique fact in history that, amidst the vicissitudes of centuries, St. John Lateran still possesses a farm, that of Cento-Celle, which was a gift of the conqueror of Maxentius.

The gifts of Pepin, of Charlemagne, of other Carlovingians to the same metropolis, are not more doubtful. Those of Louis XI., of Henry IV., and of the Governments which have succeeded one another in France since 1801, rest upon equally authentic titles; as you are well aware.

Since the Middle Ages, the domains of this cathedral mistress of all churches were distinguished in public acts and diplomas by the words *Solum Laterannense*, the soil of the Lateran. By an identical expression the 5th art. of your Law of Guarantees still terms them ' *the soil of the Lateran.*'

But this venerable antiquity, which surrounds them with a halo of majesty, and which consecrates them, as a Roman writer formerly said, *Vetera quædam majestas consecrat*, does not inspire you with the smallest respect. The patrimony even of St. John Lateran is at this moment threatened.

But it is not only to the emperors and Christian monarchs that the patrimony of the Roman Church owes its origin. History records numerous and important donations made, since the first centuries of the Church, by the faithful of every class and of every land in favour of St. Peter and his successors. Under all circumstances and in a variety of forms, these donations have succeeded one another without interruption. To these gifts were added, in proportion as the Church developed itself, the contributions of the Catholic world, reserves of benefices, annual consistorial dues, produce of tribunals for dispensations, of secretaryships of briefs, fines of kingdoms which are fiefs of the Church, and Peter's pence : all revenues coming from without.

Is there the smallest doubt, sir, of this fact ? Is it to Rome as an Italian municipality, or to Catholic Rome, the common home of Christians, that the whole world has granted annual consistorial dues, paid for vacant benefices, sent the produce of subscriptions and contributions from all the provinces of the religious orders to enrich so many magnificent buildings, consecrated by religion and all the marvels which have there been accumulated ? Every one knows that the Roman States gave very little to the Popes; it was only towards the second half of the fifteenth century that direct taxes of any sort were imposed; older, but purely local, the indirect taxes were so slight that they hardly sufficed to defray the current expenses of the municipality.

The revenues of the Popes, not as temporal but **as spiritual** sovereigns, were, on the contrary, very considerable ; and it is with these revenues that in all times they have founded pious establishments, built splendid monuments, and made Rome a city worthy of being the capital of the whole Christian world.

It is a matter of public notoriety that the cardinals likewise had formerly very large incomes, and that the greater part of them made the noblest use of these resources ; as their magnificent foundations and beautiful churches and chapels so clearly attest.

If it be so, then—if the property of the Roman Church has, in its largest portion, a foreign origin, the largesses of Catholicity itself—is it not evident, sir, that these possessions do not belong to Italy ? and that this Catholic Rome, enriched by the gifts of the whole Christian world, and the prodigious riches, both artistic and monumental, which she contains, can in no way be considered as your lawful prey, to be disposed of at your convenience or according to your will and pleasure ?

That is the reason why what you are doing, silently and in the dark—I mean, the operations of your ' giunta liquidatrice' and the spoliations which are being carried on, or are in preparation—are things which concern us in the highest degree ; and we cannot, without protesting from the very bottom of our consciences, see you thus quietly appropriating sacred treasures which belong to ourselves.

This, then, is the whole truth. The Italian Government has deceived the Catholic world by a series of promises which it has not kept. It has despoiled and is despoiling the Roman Church more and more, day by day, and in the most disgraceful manner. It has destroyed its exterior position and very existence, and accumulated ruins upon ruins. In one word, of which you must feel more than any one the full bearing, and against which accusation your colleagues protested in vain, *una ripresa del fisco*, of this you must bear the shame. The occupation of Rome is simply that, and nothing else : *una ripresa del fisco*.

In common honesty, I again ask you, can you flatter yourself, after all this, that you have kept your promises, and thus responded to ' THE CONFIDENCE OF EUROPE AND THE EXPECTATION OF THE CATHOLIC WORLD' ?

VII.

Blows dealt to the Priesthood and to Religion itself.

If, from the spectacle of this immense spoliation, we turn to another, that of the disorganisation of the Church, and the blows dealt by the Italian Government against the spiritual administration of the Holy Father, as well as against religion itself, the sight, sir, is more heart-breaking still. Here we must give up illusions or attempts to deceive the Church and the world by appearances. Here, more than anywhere else, we can prove the powerlessness of your words.

Yes, what really confounds me, sir, is less the hardihood of your acts than that of your affirmations, so manifestly contrary to your anterior formal declarations, to the evidence of our senses, and to the daily facts before our eyes.

What is the state of the clergy in Italy? What gaps have not already been made in her bosom, thus striking out the very life of the Church at its source!

This is one of the inevitable consequences of your laws of spoliation.

The monks and religious orders in Italy administered a great number of parishes. By suppressing them you have disturbed the whole parochial system. How? you ask. Cannot they continue to serve the parishes? Yes; but they die every day, and death during the twenty-five years of your revolution has been busy in their ranks. And after them? You are perfectly well aware that you have made novitiates impossible.

The secular clergy even, how are they to be recruited, with your hard military law and endless vexations?

The property of the seminaries has also been liquidated, reduced by 30 per cent, and subjected to extraordinary taxation. It is the Holy Father who gives them a subsidy from Peter's pence, and thus alone prevents their perishing.

You do not even exempt from military service the young pupils of the sanctuary destined for the altar! Never has such a thing been done by any people; but it is done by you.

Will you tell me that the law enables them to purchase a substitute? But at what price? A ransom of 3500 francs (140*l.* English). In the actual state of the finances of the

c

Church, who do you expect can pay such a ransom? You were quite sure, by this means, to disorganise and empty all the great seminaries.

In a college of one hundred students, there would then be 350,000 francs to provide, independently of other expenses of keep, food, and education. Where on earth could such a sum be raised? In the actual resources of the Church? You have one hundred and twenty bishops who do not receive a farthing from the State.

The Archbishop of Turin is reduced to living in a tiny room in his own seminary.

The Archbishop of Pisa the same. I have visited them both. And how many more!

A ransom of 3500 francs! and even after paying it, one only passes from the first category of the contingent to the second.*

To escape from the rigour of your military laws, a good many young priests took refuge in provinces which had not yet been annexed. After the annexation, you hunted them out, seized them, and, notwithstanding the sacred character with which they were invested, you incorporated them by main force into your regiments. It is a well-known and undoubted fact that, at the siege of Rome in 1870, the army of invasion contained a large number of these poor priests, who, once in Rome, used to go secretly into the sacristies, and tear off for half an hour their hateful military costume, so as to be able once more to celebrate the Holy Sacrifice!

Yes, this indignity, sir, has been a sad reality. The dearth of priests is already great: I do not know the actual number of parishes which have no priests, but I know that it is already fearful. I have been told of one diocese in Italy where, out of one hundred and fifty cures, there are seventy vacant.

What will it be in a few years? Then, public worship having ceased, for want of priests, in a great number of churches, both at Rome and throughout Italy, it is frightful to think what will become of these sanctuaries, and still more of those souls!

But, besides, is not the incessant, relentless war declared

---

* 'Legge sulle basi generali per l' organamento dell' exercito,' art. 4.

against the clergy, the Pope, and religion itself, in spite of your attempts to dissimulate the fact, but too well known ?

Do you not make every effort to deprive the children of the poor of any religious instruction ? 'The Pope free,' you say, 'in a free State.' Free, yes, to bear every attack, every threat, every outrage.

The dupe—I will not say the accomplice—of the declared enemies of religion, of those who own loudly that their object is to *unchristianise* Rome and Italy, the Italian Government permits everything—in the press, on the bookstalls, at the theatre, even in the streets ! Remember the coarse, public, and impious sacrileges which remained unpunished at the time of the last Roman carnival.

I have seen the most impious and odious caricatures exposed on the walls of the capital of the Catholic world.

There is not a single nation, even of those separated from the Church, who would tolerate similar scandals. I do not even except Geneva. I have seen in Rome itself, in libraries of recent date, some stuck even at the back of the walls of the churches, horrible little books, very cheap, in which our dogmas, our worship, the Papacy, the Episcopate, the clergy, are treated with the most contemptuous ridicule, and loaded with the vilest calumnies. I have seen at the doors of these libraries enormous advertisements offering books to the passers-by such as this, *Anatomia del Papismo !*

And the Pope is compelled to witness such scandals, and is powerless to suppress them.

Yes, sir, you are dealing heavy blows, not only against the faith, but against the morals of this Roman population; as if you only hoped to drag from their hearts their well-known fidelity to the Holy Father by throwing them into an abyss of corruption and apostasy.

But we will now go on to show what is the nature of the attacks levelled against the spiritual administration of the Holy Father, and against the public services of the universal Church.

VIII.

Destruction of the Roman College.

You have destroyed the Roman College. But what was

the Roman College? An Italian establishment? No. It was an institution essentially Catholic, a school of theology for the whole world. Rome is the centre of faith and doctrine. It is important to the whole Catholic world that from every land the bishops should be able to send their future priests to classes where, with the highest authority, under the eyes of the Supreme Pontiff himself, ecclesiastical science should be taught. That is why, in execution of the decrees of the Council of Trent, the Popes founded these seminaries in Rome : a diocesan seminary, the Apollinare, for the priests of the Roman Church, and a seminary for the whole Catholic world—*omnium gentium seminarium*—the Roman College ; a college which from the hour of its foundation has been international ; international by the decrees of Gregory XIII., from the professors who taught in it, and from the various nationalities and origin of the students who frequent it, and have frequented it for the last three centuries. It is there also that in our days the seminaries of the different nations, and the rectors of the English, Irish, Scotch, Belgian, American, French, and German colleges, sent their students in order to perfect them in their studies, with masters who reckoned among their body the most illustrious representatives of the sacred sciences.

Well, what have you done with this grand and noble institution? From the moment of your entry into Rome, in September 1870, you invaded the halls of this college, you forbade the Roman youth to frequent it, you diminished by one half the salaries which the Sovereign Pontiff had awarded to the professors ; and then, on the 8th October 1873, you definitively suppressed the whole university.

You promised, it is true, another locality and the continuance of the salary of the professors, reduced by you to one half ; but you have awarded neither salary nor any fresh locality. The rectors of the foreign colleges have claimed the fulfilment of your promise, and applied to the *giunta liquidatrice*. They have not even had a word of answer. Therefore, there is no longer a hall for the classes, no longer any salaries for the professors.

You have, therefore, taken possession of the magnificent buildings of the Roman College, which were founded for the whole of Christianity; then, in order the more effectually to ruin this great institution of Catholic education—not daring to lay your hands on the colleges of foreign nations, because you would have had to reckon with those nations—you have condemned the students of these colleges to wander here and there in Rome to seek a shelter for their professors and for themselves. At last they were enabled, at great expense, to establish themselves in a hired house. But then you, under the pretext that these classes were no longer those of the Roman College—whence you yourselves have banished them —you have actually suppressed the whole of the salaries of the professors, which had already been, as I said before, reduced by one half! The rectors of the different foreign colleges addressed to you fresh remonstrances, and again claimed your promise. *No answer.* The Holy Father then took up the cause, and claimed restitution; so did the bishops, the professors, the rectors of colleges — even directly to yourself, M. Minghetti! You never deigned to give the smallest response. You keep the buildings of the Roman College, which is ours by right, and you pocket the 12,000 Roman scudi which was assigned to the professors by the Pontifical Government.

In thus destroying, in spite of the protests of the Pope and the Episcopate, this illustrious college, the fruit of three centuries, you have ignored the sacred rights of the Pope, the Bishops, and the Catholic Powers; you have thrown immense difficulties in the way of instruction in the sacred sciences; and you have injured in the highest degree the spiritual and scientific interests of Catholicity itself.

This, again, is the way in which you have fulfilled your engagements, respected your Law of Guarantees, and striven TO SOLVE THE ROMAN QUESTION WITHOUT WOUNDING THE FEELINGS OF THE CATHOLIC WORLD.

IX.

Destruction of the Mother-houses of the Religious Orders.

The Law, so called, of *Guarantees*, voted by the Italian Parliament on the 13th of May 1871, is founded on the principle that the Pope is *entirely free to accomplish the functions of his spiritual ministry.* These are the exact terms of the 9th art.

This law recognises, still further, ' that he cannot fulfil the functions of his ministry alone, and that *the Church is necessarily a secular body served by Regular Orders.*' And the first thing you-did was to destroy these Regular Orders. Can there be a more flagrant contradiction ? And at this very moment you are putting the corner-stone to your work, by destroying the mother-houses of these Orders. There were grouped round the Holy See certain mother-houses, centres of government for those numerous communities of workers disseminated throughout the Christian world. There the generals of these Orders resided, with their respective councils : and thus the whole body of the Religious Orders found themselves in constant and direct communication with the Head of the Church.

And not only did the principal heads of the great Orders reside near the Holy See, with which they had constant relations, but a link was thus formed between the metropolitan houses of the Order, and the other houses under their government. It was in these mother-houses that the religious of different monasteries, who were sent to Rome on various affairs, received hospitality ; and in them also were held the chapters and assemblies of the heads of all the different provinces of each Order, when there was a question of the election of a new superior-general. Such convents, therefore, are on a totally different footing in Rome from other places. There they are only private establishments, without any absolutely necessary relation to the rest of Catholicity, and generally founded with the money of particular countries or individuals. They might even cease to exist, without any radical blow being struck at the government of the Church towards the *religious institutions*, which everywhere she must direct. But at Rome the convents are quite another thing, and by striking at them in the centre or heart of the Church, you have done an irreparable injury to institutions which are of vital interest to the whole of Catholicity, and which were created not only for this universal end, but with funds to which the population of the Pontifical States have contributed little or nothing.

O, I know very well that even here you have tried to conceal your acts under certain forms, and proceeded with apparent moderation; you have not denied in principle—you have even formally recognised—the necessity of a representation of the great Orders around the Pope; and in the law which extends to the province of Rome the destruction of the Religious Orders in Italy, you have specified the sum which should be granted to the Holy Father for the maintenance of the representatives of the great Orders about his person (art. 3, no. 4); you have even given to the King's Government the *faculty* to leave to the representatives of the great Orders, who have houses in foreign nations, the necessary localities for their own residence and the performance of their functions. But for how long a time? As long as they hold that office; *fino à che dura l' ufficio loro*. And afterwards?

In the mean while they have been forced to evacuate their own mother-houses. You have turned them out of doors, and installed yourselves in their place. And what is to become of these generals or procurators-general of the Religious Orders, isolated and wandering, reduced to the most precarious means of existence, exposed, if of foreign nationality, to falling under the power of the police, and to be no more than tolerated on Italian territory: deprived also of all the resources which they formerly possessed in their communities?

And then you are surprised, after such a violation of your most formal promises, after such attacks against the dearest interests of the Pope and the Church, that a cry rises up against you from the heart of every Catholic in Europe?

X.

Disorganisation of the Roman Congregations.

I reminded you just now, that in your Law of Guarantees, art. 9, you were forced to admit that ' the Pope could not accomplish alone the functions of his spiritual ministry.' What an immense administration, in truth, is that of the universal Church! The religious of the whole world flock for reference in their affairs to Rome. From Rome comes the impulse which is communicated to the farthest extremities of Catholicity. This vast government has necessitated the creation of numberless congregations, true ministers of the Church, who surround the Holy See, and between whom all the affairs of the Church are divided. Of all the kingdoms of the earth, the Pontifical administration is that which listens the most carefully to councils. If, in the last stage of any act of importance, the Pope personally examines the question, nothing can be less arbitrary than his decision. All questions, before being finally resolved on by him, have been carefully studied, meditated, and discussed by this legion of counsellors who fill the Roman congregations, and which are presided over by the cardinals.

We should add that the Pope necessarily has his nuncios, his legates, his inter-nuncios, and his *chargés d'affaires*, to be his representatives both with the Churches and the foreign Governments.

It is evident that, to suffice for such an administration, Rome requires an ecclesiastical body of the highest order ; a nursery of men trained for a long while to fill such posts, well versed in all political and religious questions, and broken in to public business.

Well, the religious life, more than any other ecclesiastical position, the quiet of the cloister, aided by libraries and archives, facilitates all those vast researches which are required for a thorough knowledge of theology, canon law, and ecclesiastical history; and far more than secular priests, absorbed by the duties of the ministry, these hidden workers are thoroughly versed in the difficult causes which are frequently confided to them.

That is one of the reasons why the Religious Orders had so large a share in these congregations, and the members furnished by them were neither the least learned nor the least laborious of those whom the Pope called to his aid in the government of the Church.

Henceforth, how will he be able to provide for so numerous a body ? And how prepare men to whom such learned and onerous functions are to be intrusted, if they no longer possess houses, or monasteries, or places of meeting to shelter not only themselves, but their archives and libraries ? If the Church have no longer any certain property, nor any establishment which she can securely possess, where can she educate the men she wants, and offer to those who are preparing for the ministry, for missions, ecclesiastical judgeships, or professorships of education, peaceful shelters or special resources for preparation for their respective vocations? And when, notwithstanding so many promises, you have brought about all this terrible destruction, and done such incalculable injury to the Church, you expect that the Pope, deceived and betrayed, and Catholics, indignant at the fraud put upon them, should still have confidence in your laws and your guarantees!

XI.

Menaces made to the Propaganda.

At this moment, you menace the Propaganda itself. You are beginning to sell its property. But the Propaganda, sir, is the institution the most inseparable from the Papacy, and the most necessary to Catholicity: that also which the highest interests of civilisation, no less than those of religion, command you to respect.

Euntes docete omnes gentes were the words of Christ to His Apostles on leaving them. The Pope is, if I may venture to say so, the testamentary executor of these last words of Jesus Christ.

How is it possible to admit that the Sovereign Pontiff could do without a centre for the Catholic Propaganda? To impart faith and Christian civilisation to the barbarous populations which cover the distant portions of the globe, such has always been the right and the duty of the Church. It is thus that she has carried the Gospel to the uttermost ends of the earth, and opened at the same time to all nations, in the very interest of their riches and political consideration, relations which are infinitely more precious.

And, doubtless, the work is as grand as it is laborious. We enjoy, we, old nations of the West, often with an ungrateful disdain or a proud indifference, the blessings of civilisation and Christianity: but what should we be without the Gospel? In what state are those countries on which that great light has not yet shone?

When we cast our eyes over the map of the globe, it is with a kind of stupor that we discover vast tracts still buried in heathen darkness, where the sun of faith has never yet risen. What millions of men even now, after nearly nineteen centuries of Christianity, are still idolaters, or buried in the shadows of false worship!

And what becomes of poor humanity in these sad regions? I am not even speaking of those debased races in Africa and Oceanica, who seem scarcely to deserve the name of men: I am speaking of those old civilisations in the extreme East—of those Asiatic nations, not yet Christian, but followers of Buddha and Mahomet. What an abyss of moral miseries! what deep wounds of corruption and ferocity, or of servile abjection and ignorance, unknown, by the grace of God, to people who adore Jesus Christ!

If, then, there be a work above all others most admirable, eminently Christian and civilising, is it not the work of the foreign missions? It is the immortal glory of the Catholic Church that she has never ceased to labour at them with an indefatigable zeal, and to engender in her bosom millions of apostles. Where are they not found at this very hour? What burning climate or frigid zone can arrest their zeal? What fatigues, what perils, what martyrdoms, frighten them? Wherever our travellers, our merchants, our consuls land, there the missionaries have been before them and paved the way. More than two hundred dioceses are already organised in missionary lands. I feel a pride in France when I think that, at this very moment, more than 1500 French missionaries, without counting our heroic Sisters of Charity, are labouring in the propagation of the Gospel. You will find Catholic missionaries in Europe from the highlands of Scotland and Sweden to the banks of the Danubian Provinces, and at Constantinople; in the whole of Asia, at Jerusalem, Damascus, Antioch, Beyrout, and all the cities of the Levant; then in Persia, China, Cochin China, Tonquin, Japan, in the Indies, even in Oceanica. There, the black savages of New Guinea, the Protestant colonies of Holland, the new world of Australia, the scarcely known islands of Polynesia, are full of missioners. In Africa they are labouring in Algeria, at Tunis, Tripoli, Egypt, Suez, beyond the Sahara, in Abyssinia,

Senegal, Zanzibar; in that vast Nigritia where 50,000,000 poor negroes are waiting to become men and Christians; at the Cape of Good Hope, in Madagascar, at Sierra Leone. In America you find them in New York as in Canada; even to the wild lands of Arkansas and Hudson's Bay; in Texas, at the Antilles, in Guiana—everywhere! Shall I reckon up all those orders devoted to distant missions? Lazarists, Jesuits, Dominicans, Franciscans, Passionists, the Lyons Missionaries, those of Picpus, the Marists, the Oblates of Pignerolles, the Oblates of Charity, the Sisters of St. Vincent de Paul, &c. And how many others? I stop; for it would be too long to pass in review that great and noble army of the Catholic Apostolate.

Well, who organises and directs all these missions? It is that grand Roman congregation which is called the Propaganda: that Propaganda which I might define as the Prime Minister of the Catholic missions; the first and the most indispensable of those administrations by which the Pope governs the universal Church. It is the Propaganda which, by its vicars-apostolic, governs and directs all those countries where the Catholic hierarchy is not yet regularly constituted. She is the resort of all the missionary establishments (both men and women) scattered throughout the East, in India and China, Africa, America, and the isles of the ocean; all the clergy, regular and secular, who, under one name or the other, are labouring for the propagation of the faith, are consolidated, directed, and depend entirely upon her. It is so true that Propaganda is an apostolate, not for local purposes, but for the whole world, that she does not receive students of Italian nationality. All her subjects, formed in her school, are to return to their respective orders, belonging to different countries who have sent them there.

Such is Propaganda; of all the Roman congregations, I repeat, the most considerable and the most indispensable. And it is on an institution like this, sir, that the Italian Government does not fear to lay her hands. Already has she done it an irreparable injury, as well as to all the Catholic missions, by disorganising the Religious Orders which furnished the missioners. It is to this extent, that when the eminent and zealous Cardinal Franchi, the Prefect of the

Propaganda, asked lately for some religious for an important mission in the Indies (one which first made Sanscrit known in Europe), the Cardinal failed to obtain any—their general had none left. If they be already so scarce, what will it be in the future? and where will they be able to be trained? The greater part of these orders had schools and seminaries destined to prepare for their distant apostolates those among their members who were sufficiently heroic to devote themselves to the foreign missions. These houses were provided with special libraries, and went through a special course of study for this purpose. And every one knows that it must be so. The studies of those who are to evangelise India or China must be different from those who will sail for Australia or America. Each order, besides, had certain fixed missions assigned to it. For instance, the Carmelites had, at St. Pancrazio, their seminary for the Malabar mission and the Indies; from whence, as I said just now, came the first lights which were thrown on Sanscrit, a language which is now studied throughout Europe as the mother-tongue of the Indo-Germanic tribes. The Franciscans had for their Syrian and Egyptian missions the convent of St. Bartholomew à *l'Isola*. And so with all the others. You have suppressed all these seminaries and convents; their libraries have been confiscated and scattered, and everything is disorganised and destroyed.

But now it is this great congregation of the Propaganda which the Italian Government is not afraid directly to attack. That law which subjects all the property of existing institutions to conversion into Italian funds, the Government, it appears, now wishes to apply to Propaganda itself. This would be simply to give it its death-blow.

It possesses a palace, built in the time of Urban VIII., which shelters its archives and its administration, a special college (besides those of which I spoke just now), and which is altogether dependent on Propaganda; and an immense printing establishment, for all the languages and dialects on the face of the earth. If you drive it from this palace, where do you think it could install all these things?

Its expenses are defrayed by certain houses situated in Rome, and certain lands in the Pontifical States; but how heavy would be the loss which you would make Propaganda incur by the inevitable depreciation of the value of its property, consequent on a forced sale within a limited time !

She possesses a fund of 14,000,000 or 15,000,000 francs, which gives her a revenue of 700,000 or 800,000 francs. Is it that, sir, which excites your covetousness ? Is it that which you grudge to those distant Christianities, for the maintenance of those poor and heroic missionaries who have left all to plant the Cross in pagan lands ? Do you consider that it is too much for the immense and magnificent work of the apostolate and of civilisation which the Propaganda accomplishes?

How much do you think that England gives every year for her Protestant missions? 20,000,000 francs. And Russia, to propagate her schism ? 4,000,000 francs. Propaganda has less than 1,000,000 francs for the diffusion of the Gospel. And on these meagre and sacred resources, sacred twice over in the eyes of humanity as in those of religion, you would dare to lay your hands !

What ! you have in Rome such a fountain of light and civilisation, the very centre of the great Catholic Apostolate ; an institution which sends Gospel missionaries everywhere, that is, civilisation ; which has rendered, and is still rendering, such incalculable services to European diplomacy, to commerce, to letters, to science—and you do not feel proud of such an honour ? And you do not wish to preserve so glorious a privilege ? And you do not see that to touch a similar institution would be to dishonour you in the eyes, not only of Christianity, but of all civilised nations ?

XII.

The War declared against lay scientific Institutions.

After all, to what lengths do you not push your interference and that passion for subjecting everything to the tyranny of the State ? Of this the war you have declared against the lay scientific institutions of Rome is only another proof. There are at Rome learned bodies and illustrious academics, founded by the Popes or under their patronage, whose members are either first-rate artists or savans of the first class: academics which have their laws, their franchises, their autonomies, which have always been respected by the wisdom and magnanimity of the Sovereign Pontiffs. This independence, so honourable to science, so favourable to true progress, gives umbrage to your Government : it has determined to destroy them. It will be to the eternal honour of these Roman academies that they are still struggling courageously against these illiberal invasions. But to what poor vexations, what miserable proceedings, have you not had recourse against them ! Thus, with the most ancient, the most celebrated of all these academies, the Academy of Fine Arts of St. Luke—founded under the express condition, which the Popes have always accepted and respected, that she should be absolute mistress of her own patrimony and supreme in her own interior government—you want to compel her to change her statutes, and even her name ! She resists. I have read with admiration, I own, her noble and proud revindication of her secular rights. I know nothing more honourable to science than this protestation, drawn up by M. Betti, signed by twenty professors, and addressed by them to your Minister of Public Instruction.

The professors of the Roman University remained faithful to the Pontiff. To make them expiate this fidelity, what have you imagined ? To compel them to take the political oath to the Government. Never had the Popes exacted such an oath. You yourselves had not asked it of the professors of the University of Padua.

After your entry into Rome, you hastened to exact this oath from the Padua professors, so as to have some colour for forcing it on the Roman University. To the honour of the Sovereign Pontiff and the confusion of your Government, what happened ? The greater part of them, and those the most celebrated, absolutely refused, and in consequence lost their professorial chairs.

The Archæological Academy unanimously voted to retain her title of *Pontificale*, and to maintain her right of free election of her president. To punish her, you have not blushed to withdraw from this learned body the modest pension of 3000 francs, which the State allowed her for her annual expenses, and to drive her from the halls of the university where she held her sittings.

You saw also that the majority of the *Lincei Pontificii* voted for the retention of this title of *Pontificii*, which they naturally hold in honour: you compelled this majority to give way to a small minority.

But there has been found an upright and honourable man, the Prince Buoncompagni, whose science and erudition are known to all Europe, and who, at his own cost, publishes the reports of their meetings: so that, in spite of you, the *Lincei Pontificii* continue to exist.

XIII.

That the Spoliation of the Church has not enriched Italy.

Well, you have despoiled the Church. Are you any the richer ? You have thrown this prey into the yawning gulf of your empty exchequer : has this gulf been, in consequence, filled up ? No; it has been made wider.

It has often been remarked that the property of the Church never brings any luck to those who take possession of it. ' Woe,' exclaims Bossuet, ' be to those who lay their hands upon it !' Look at Spain and so many other nations, whom such robbery has neither saved from bankruptcy, nor from invasion, nor from the disaster of *assignats*.

You have come to this—to paper-money.

What has become of all the property of the Church in Italy? Who has profited by it? Who has swallowed it up?

What I know is, that the deficit in your finances swells each year to gigantic proportions, and the taxes and the National Debt likewise. Your budget exceeds by 730,000,000 francs (that is, by more than half) the budgets of all the Italian States taken together before the union.

That is to say, Italian unity costs to-day 730,000,000 francs to the Italians.

The increase of the expenditure year by year is, according to an expression of the Deputy Corbetta, something enormous, something quite incredible ('qualche cosa di enorme, qualche cosa d' incredibile'). In truth :

In 1868 (it is from the same Deputy Corbetta that I borrow the figures), the budget of expenditure was 998,000,000;

in 1869, 1,100,000,000; in 1870, 1,111,000,000; in 1871, 1,498,000,000; and this year 1874, it was 1,528,000,000.*

Naturally, taxation follows in a continually ascending scale, but it does not suffice; and so each year the deficit increases and the debt becomes larger.

In 1861, the deficit was 39,000,000; in 1871, 84,232,761; in 1872, 233,019,199.

In 1861, the public debt of Italy was 111,000,000 (I speak of the interest); in 1871, it was 440,000,000, representing a capital of 10,000,000,000.

How, besides, can we be astonished at this deficit in the budget and constant increase of the debt, when on a budget of 1,309,000,000 of receipts for the year 1872, one must deduct from it, first, for the interest of the debt, guarantees, and dotations, a share of 931,160,059, on which no economy is possible?

Thus the debt is always increasing—always, always—and the taxes too.

It has been proved that, before 1860, the average tax paid in Italy by each inhabitant was only 19 francs 83 centimes, including the provincial and municipal taxes. In 1873, each inhabitant paid on an average 44 francs 63 centimes; that is, since 1861 the tax is more than doubled.

With the spur of this debt and the necessity of this taxation, the demands of the Italian fiscal system have become something prodigious.

I have been told of one college in Rome, which before 1870 paid 300 francs in taxes to the Pontifical Government; this same college pays you now 3800.

I know one private individual, whose fortune does not amount to more than an honest competence, and who now has to pay in Rome 9000 francs for a house which was formerly taxed at 400 francs.

The difference between 400 and 9000 francs seems incredible; but it has been carefully proved to me.

Our pious establishments, as I before said, paid the Pontifical Government 11,500 francs.

To-day they pay 28,000, and probably very soon they will have to pay 34,000.

* These sums are given in francs.

Such is the progress of taxation.

Now, if we look into this subject in detail, what shall we find? Ah, your financiers are men of expedients, sir, and your unity costs Italy dear.

A deputy has lately proved before the Chambers that a bit of bread, before it can be eaten, has paid twenty-one different taxes!

What did you not say against the Popes on the subject of the tax on the grinding of corn? A very moderate one, besides.

To-day this tax is not only doubled and trebled, but it has been extended to all kinds of flour, to Indian corn, to chestnuts, to haricots; that is, to all those articles which form the food of the poor.

And as to the rents of houses, how do you proceed? Do you levy the tax on the real price of the lodging, which is a thoroughly equitable proceeding? No; but on a fictitious rent, which you yourselves have fixed.

'Here,' exclaims the owner of a house, 'is what my house brings me in. Here is the tenant's lease.' 'Ah,' you reply, 'it is your fault if you do not let it for more. You can let it for so much; you will pay accordingly; put more pressure upon your lodgers.'

The mother of a family, in consequence of arrangements made with her children, received from them, in exchange for a cession of her property, a life annuity; the Pontifical Government had never thought of taxing this kind of annuity, as the property in return for which this annuity was paid had already been taxed; but you hastened at once to levy a tax upon it. I know a Roman lady who pays you on this account 12,000 francs.

A poor priest towards the ends of March comes to present his life-certificate, in order to draw his very small pension. You ask him for his certificates for the end of February and January. Certainly, as he was alive at the end of March, there was no doubt that he was equally alive in February and January. But they did it to force him to pay for three stamps instead of one.

I must stop. Facts of this sort are innumerable. What conclusion can we draw from them? This—that in despoil-

D

ing the Church you have not enriched Italy. But if you have not enriched her, have you done her honour ?

XIV.

Is the Spoliation of the Church just in Principle? Has the Church the Right to possess Property?

I will not leave this sad subject without setting forth one last question—the general question of principle. Many will smile, sir, at this vindication of rights which will never prevent the use of might against right. But for the honour of humanity there are certain fundamental truths that the world cannot be allowed to proscribe ; and so, however importunate or superfluous my protest may appear, I shall make it.

I will no longer speak of your engagements or your promises. I will only speak of the nature of things and eternal justice. Had you the right to take from the Church what you have done ?

No. You had not.

Notwithstanding all the sophistry invented in favour of every usurpation, it is needful to maintain and proclaim, sir, this truth : that the Church has by herself, and by the sole fact of her Divine institution and existence, the right to possess; an essential right, at the same time natural and Divine, which Governments are bound to recognise and to guard by careful and protective legislation, but which they never have the right to paralyse, to destroy, and still less to confiscate for their own profit.

She has the right to possess, and why? Because she has the right to live. Because she exists, and because One greater than you has established her on the earth.

Whoever has the right of existence here below has the right of property ; these two rights are essentially co-relative.

Do not reply that the Church is a spiritual society. However spiritual the Church may be in her Divine institution, she is not hung up in the air. She is founded upon the earth and for the inhabitants of the earth. *Teach all nations : preach the Gospel to every creature.* She is in the world and for the world ; she is composed of men ; she needs for her mission, for her works, for her worship, for her temples, for her clergy, certain resources, without which she could not provide for the necessities of her existence. And the slightest reflection will be enough to convince you that the right of property can alone insure these resources for certain, without which her liberty would always be precarious and her existence miserably dependent.

Yes; to deny to the Church the right of possession, you must also deny to her the right of existence; and, in fact, it is this radical and impious negation which is at the root of all the systems hostile to ecclesiastical property. In spite, then, of all the sophistries, ancient and modern, the truth, the irreversible truth, is there.

And the facts here confirm the principles. This right is so completely a necessity, it is so true that the Church, from the moment of her existence, can and ought to hold property, that, in fact, she has everywhere and always possessed it.

It is uncontestable, that under the pagan emperors themselves, the Christians, the Christian Churches, and especially the Roman Church, had properties which were both acknowledged and respected. Mother and mistress of all the churches, the Church of Rome was, from the very first, as she ought to be, and long before Constantine, the richest in resources, the most powerful in action, and the most profuse in her liberality. The monuments, the most illustrious acts, teach us that the Roman Church, which had to provide for such a multitude of other wants, possessed not only a quantity of furniture of the highest value, but also considerable funds.

The history of the foundations of all the Churches in Europe and throughout the world proves that there was not a single great Christian community which had not, and was not compelled to have, possessions more or less important. Excepting during the storms of persecution, the emperors and the pagan magistrates not only recognised this right of property in the Christian Church, but often protected it against the injustice and violence of its usurpers. Thus, when Paul of Samosata at Antioch remained, in spite of the condemnation of a council, through the protection of Queen Zenobia, in a house belonging to the Church, Aurelian, on the complaint of the Christians, ordered that the house should be adjudged to those to whom the Bishops of Italy and the Roman Pontiffs should address their letters; so clearly was it admitted, even by the pagans, that the Christian Church had the right to possess, and notoriously that the mark of a true Christian was communion with the Roman Church. Lampsidius, in his Life of Alexander Severus, recounts with minute details how this emperor insisted on a certain spot, of which the possession was disputed, being given back to the Christians for the exercise of their religious worship. Who does not know the famous decree by which Constantine and Licinius ordered 'the restitution to the Christian Churches of all that had belonged to them—*omnia quæ ad Ecclesias recte visa fuerint pertiner*—houses, fields, gardens, all the property, in a word, of which the late persecutions had deprived them'?[*]

'We hereby order and decree, as regards the Christians, that if the sites where they have been used before to meet have been bought by any one, *whether out of our exchequer or from whatever other person*, they shall be immediately restored to the Christians. All these sites shall incontinently be delivered to the *community, that is, to the churches, and not to individuals;* you will give back all these things to their communities as a body.'

It therefore was a recognised thing, in the very midst of paganism, that the Church had a right of property; that very right which men, calling themselves Catholics, dare after eighteen centuries of Christianity to contest and deny.

But if the Church have the right to possess, the legitimate property of the Church is as sacred and inviolable as any other property. I defy you to invoke, in order to justify your usurpation, a principle which would not overthrow the rights of all property—that is, of society itself.

And wherefore, I would again ask, should the property of the Church—that is, property which comes from savings and toil, sanctified by abnegation and sacrifice; property which, after all, is more consecrated to God, to souls, and to the

---

[*] 'Omnia ergo quæ ad Ecclesias recte visa fuerint pertinere, sive domus, ac possessio sit, sive agri, sive horti, sive quæcumque alia, nullo jure quod ad dominium pertinet imminuto, sed salvis omnibus atque integrio manentibus, restitui jubemus.' Eusebius, *Vita Constant.* lib. ii. cap. 39.

universal good of the human race than any other—why, I ask, should its possession be less legitimate, less sacred, less inviolable, than riches born of speculation, of commerce, of industry, of credit, of the employment of capital ?

The words of Bossuet remain, then : ' It is an unheard-of injustice to wish to profit by the spoils of this daughter of the King of kings . . . Her God will Himself take her quarrel in hand, and will be a rude Avenger on those who have dared to lay their sacrilegious hands upon her.'

XV.

Conclusion.

I pause and conclude.

Doubtless I am far from having said all regarding the spoliation and oppression of the Church at Rome and throughout Italy.   If, however, sir, I have been led into any error of detail, I am quite ready to own it publicly and to disavow it. I only wish for truth, and for truth the most indubitable. But the substance of the picture I have drawn will not less subsist, and suffices to prove the justice of those complaints which the Holy Father vented in his last Encyclical :

' With a criminal skill they deprive us bit by bit of all those means and aids which render possible the government of the Church.   Who does not now see clearly how false was the assertion, that, by the usurpation of our capital, the liberty of the Roman Pontiff, in the exercise of his spiritual power and his relations with the Catholic world, has not been diminished ?'*

Before this sad and sorrowful reality, I find myself filled with many thoughts.   But I must bury them in my own breast, for we are living in days when, as Tacitus said of old, ' Even groaning is not free—*Gemitus liber non fuit.*'   Still

* ' Per nefarias arte paulatim nobis subducuntur præsidia et instrumenta quibus Ecclesiam universam regere ac moderari valeamus ; luculenter patet quantum a veritate abhorreat quod affirmatum fuit, nihil esse imminutum. Urbe nobis adempta de libertate Romani Pontificis in exercitio spiritualis ministerii et in iis agendis quæ ad Catholicum pertinent orbum.' *Encycl.* of Nov. 20, 1873.

less are we free to vindicate those imprescriptable rights for which I have always fought; but they remain immortal in our hearts and consciences.

What, however, stands out plainly in this sad state of things is this: That the Roman question is not solved. And it is important that neither Italy nor Europe, any more than Catholics themselves, should be under illusion on this point.

The consequences of this abnormal position of the Papacy have not yet developed themselves; but are we to wait till they all burst forth? And what mind which is at all clear-sighted can fail to foresee them?

This is what I conjure, I do not say only sincere Catholics, but all serious statesmen and all the real friends of Italy, to consider.

Yes; there is in the present state of things a cause of immense and permanent moral perturbation for the whole world. Those who believe that might is right, and who fancy that they will easily overcome Catholicity, may here affect indifference or disdain. But those who know the place which the destinies of this great Church and those of the Pope, its Supreme Head, still hold in the human mind, and what may be at any given moment, the power of sacred resistance and the invincible reclamations of souls, those have no doubt as to the inevitable perils before which we are blindly running, by leaving the Papacy in a state of dependence which is intolerable, and suffering the highest interests of Christians to be jeopardised by our indifference.

It is likewise evident that this antagonism between Italy and the Church throws Italy completely out of her proper path, and that such a policy is no less contrary to her true interests than to her history; to her future than to her past; and I may add to the wishes of her population, who are deeply religious.

No; if the Papacy was and is, according to the word of the illustrious Rossi, the greatest grandeur of Italy, the Papacy and Italy are not made to be at war with one another. History, or rather Providence—it is again an illustrious Italian, the eloquent Balbo, who proclaims it—has placed between their destinies a glorious and inseparable solidarity. The present rupture is a deplorable aberration, which will become more fatal to Italy than to the Church.

That is what the voice of its wise men is for ever crying out; that is what centuries attest; that is what is prophesied of the definitive issue of all the struggles against the Papacy.

Let Italy begin, then, to think seriously; and let her pause in the path down which the revolutionary fever is dragging her; yes, let her ponder over these things; for the eyes of Christian Europe cannot always, nor for long together, be turned away from Rome and her Pontiff.

The day when the extreme consequences of the state to which the Papacy has been reduced are made manifest, if the unforeseeing and guilty people of Italy allow things to go so far,—on that day she will gather, but too late, the bitter fruits of the policy of which to-day she is so proud. Then Europe will remember her duties towards the Papacy, which are, in reality, her duties towards herself.

Then, whether we will or not, we shall have to look to the security of consciences, to the troubles of souls, to the pacification of the Church; but would it not be wiser, is it not, in fact, most urgent to prevent, if possible, the inevitable difficulties into which we shall have been thrown? The longer we wait, the more complicated becomes the problem.

Italy itself laid down the principle of a diplomatic understanding with the Powers possessing Catholic subjects. Let the Powers remind her of this, if she has already forgotten it. The interests of the whole world are concerned in it. There, indeed, might be found a solution of the question. If only the counsels of wisdom should prevail—if only Italy and Europe would look before them! Whatever may happen, we have faith in the future. The pacific triumph of the Church will come—that is our firm hope. But when? how? after what misfortune? This is God's secret.

We earnestly entreat, however, the good-will of men to help Providence in this case. If they refuse, Providence *farà da se*. The last word will be surely with her.

An Italian deputy lately invoked at the tribune *Eternal Justice*. He was badly received. But never mind. Eternal Justice exists; and sooner or later she will have her day.

It is that which makes me hopeful; and I will hope against all hope.

Such, sir, are the reflections which I have thought it right to lay before you. You see, as I said at the beginning, that I make no appeal to the sword. No; I only appeal to the instincts of a wise policy, to patriotism, and lastly, to the consciences of honest men. Permit me also to add, sir, that I make an appeal likewise to your own personal feelings. Remember the venerable Pontiff, of whom you were the Minister, who trusted in you, and whom Providence has led through such bitter reverses to a grand old age, beyond even the years of Peter, to give to the world the prolonged spectacle of the most magnanimous resignation in misfortune, and also to keep the door always open to repentance and hope.

Accept, sir, the homage of all my sentiments,

FELIX, Bishop of Orleans.

THE POPE'S BRIEF TO THE BISHOP OF ORLEANS,

ON THE OCCASION OF HIS LETTER TO M. MINGHETTI.

Pius IX. Pontiff.

Venerable Brother, greeting and apostolic benediction.

Although the extreme impudence with which the most sacred engagements are each day flagrantly violated by the men who govern Italy has, here and there, roused the anger and complaints of all honest men, and even of newspapers who are hostile to religion, nevertheless, venerable brother, we think that you have lately done the most useful and opportune work by unveiling the whole series of solemn promises made by these same men to deceive the people, and avert the indignation of the Catholic Powers; and by a plain statement of facts, demonstrating the flagrant violation of all these promises. Doubtless, as you have yourself well said, it is not this which will put a stop to the audacity of men without faith, or draw from their torpor those who, by allowing such iniquities to be accomplished unpunished, are preparing their own destruction. Nevertheless, when these facts are gathered together, arranged in order, and placed side by side with their promises, as they are in your Letter, it is impossible that such a statement should not strike those who read it, and, if they have not lost all moral sense, make them execrate such infamy and audacity.

We congratulate you, therefore, on having employed the noble gifts which God has bestowed upon you of talent, laborious activity, and eloquence, to drag from the foreheads of these men the mask *of legality* with which they strive to cover themselves each time that they are plotting some fresh injustice or some new iniquity.

It is not, in fact, a slight wound inflicted on evil when you can lay bare its infamy in the face of day.

Whatever may happen, without any doubt your writing is of a nature, while confirming and strengthening honest men, to open the eyes of many who have hitherto been deceived or misled ; and perhaps it may give birth to a salutary shame in the hearts of some of our enemies, and induce them to withdraw from the false and culpable path in which they are engaged.

We ask instantly of God that your writing may obtain such a result : and as a pledge of Divine favour and of our particular affection we impart to you, from the bottom of our heart, venerable brother, both to you and to your diocese, our apostolic benediction.

Given at St. Peter's in Rome the 19th October 1874, in the twenty-ninth year of our Pontificate.

PIE IX. POPE.

PIUS PAPA IX.

Venerabilis frater, salutem et apostolicam benedictionem.

Licet effrons impudentia, qua data publice fides quotidie frangitur audacius ab Italiæ moderatoribus passim excitaverit vituperationem et querelas honestorum omnium, imo et interdum ipsarum quoque ephemeridum religioni infensarum ;

per opportunum tamen opus et perutile te fecisse censemus, venerabilis frater, dum et solemnium promissionum seriem explicasti ab iis editarum ad decipiendum populum, continendamque potentium indignationem; et hisce objecisti facta flagrantissimam exhibentia violationem singularum. Id sane, uti scite animadvertisti, nec horumce veteratorum ausum cohibebit, nec torporem excutiet ab iis qui, hæc impune fieri sinentes, sibi ipsis parant exitium; collectæ tamen, ordinatæ, invicem oppositæ, uti sunt, ita necessario legentium mentes afficient, ut nisi animum offenderint omni prorsus exutum honestatis sensu nequeant tantæ turpitudinis et audaciæ execrationem non provocare. Gratulamur itaque, te splendidis ingenii operositatis, eloquentiæ donis a Deo largitis usum esse ad detrahendam ab istorum homiuum fronte *legalitatis* larvam, qua se abducere nituntur quoties novum aliquam fraudem machinationemque moliuntur: non leve namque vulnus infligitur vitio, dum fœditas ejus aperte revelatur. Quidquid futurum sit, lucubratio certe tua dum probos omnes confirmabit, multos illustrare poterit e deceptis, et fortasse aliquem etiam ex hostibus pudore suffundere, ac ad referendum compellere pedem a probosa semita, quam iniit. Id operi tuo potissimum adprecamur; atque interim superni favoris auspicem et præcipuæ nostræ benevolentiæ pignus apostolicam benedictionem tibi, venerabilis frater, universæque diœcesi tuæ peramanter impertimus.

Datum Romæ apud sanctum Petrum die 19 Octobris anno 1874.

Pontificatus nostri anno vicesimonono.

Pius P. IX.

LONDON:
ROBSON AND SONS, PRINTERS, PANCRAS ROAD, N.W.